THE WORLD FOLKTALE LIBRARY

Tales from the First Americans

Tales from
the First Americans

Moritz A. Jagendorf

Illustrated by Jack Endewelt

Consultant
Carolyn W. Field
Coordinator of Work with Children
The Free Library of Philadelphia

SILVER BURDETT COMPANY
Morristown, New Jersey
Glenview, Ill. • Palo Alto • Dallas • Atlanta

Library of Congress Catalog Card Number: 78-56057

INTRODUCTION

Folktales are not usually about real people or actual events, but in a way they are almost always true. They tell us something real about the people who pass them along and about their culture. Folktales often express the values of a society, or reveal that society's ideas about living and surviving. Sometimes the stories are about the joys and hopes of a people, as well as about their worries and fears. In this way, each story tells us a little about life as certain people see it.

These folktales were gathered throughout the United States from among the descendants of the first Americans. The stories were told by people who have been passing them along from generation to generation for many centuries.

In one of the stories, you will read about how the Ojibwa people explain the origin of corn, and how they learned to use it for food. Corn is a very important part of their diet. It also has an important place in their religious beliefs and in their ideas about life. If you read carefully, though, you will see that the story is about more than corn. You will learn some of the Ojibwa ideas about growing up, and about how people should behave. This story is told to young Ojibwas by the older members of the society. It is part of their education. As they listen, they learn about some of the rules of their society, as you will, while you read.

THE EDITOR

TO WEE JOHNNY

*May he never lose the rosiness
of youth, innocence, love, and friendship*

TABLE OF CONTENTS

Corn was one of the most important foods of the American Indians and there are many different stories of its origin. This is the Ojibwa tale of the creation of corn.

How Corn Came to the Indians

In the woods, long moons ago, there lived an Ojibwa Indian. He lived alone with his family because he liked to be with trees and flowers and herbs. He did not like hunting, and so his family lived mostly on fruits, berries, and roots.

This man had a son named Wunzh. Like his father, the son wanted to be with herbs and flowers. He wanted to learn how persons could use them.

Wunzh grew out of childhood. Soon he reached the age when Ojibwa boys must find a Guardian Spirit for life. He would have to live in the woods alone. There he would fast, and wait for a dream that would show him his Guardian Spirit.

His father would help, as was the tradition. He built Wunzh a hut in the woods, and the boy went there to begin his fasting. Each night he lay down hoping for his dream.

Then one night there came from the sky a young Ojibwa, dressed like none Wunzh had ever seen. His clothes were brilliant shades of green and yellow.

"The Great Spirit sent me to you," he said. "He knows of your wish to help your people. I will teach you how you can do this.

"Though your body is weak, you are strong in courage. Get up and wrestle with me to prove it."

The boy arose. With sheer strength of will, he began to wrestle with the messenger. They tested their strength for a long time, but neither won. Finally the messenger spoke again. "Enough," he said, "I will return tomorrow."

The next day the messenger came and they wrestled again. Wunzh was weaker than before. He was still fasting, and his body had only the strength of courage. But again, neither won.

"Tomorrow I will come again. You are nearing the end of your trial and you will gain your goals."

The Indian messenger came again the third day. Wunzh was very weak, but his mind and will were strong. He was determined to win.

They wrestled for a time. Then the messenger said, "Let us go into your lodge and rest, and I will teach you what to do. You have won what you desired."

They went into the lodge. There the boy listened to his Guardian Spirit. He learned about herbs and plants. After a long time the messenger said, "Tomorrow is your last day of fasting. It will be the end of your trial."

The next day the father came, bringing food. "Eat, son. You have fasted the right number of days."

"Father," he replied, "I cannot eat now. I must wait until the sun goes down. There is one more task I must do, and I must be alone." So the father left.

Exactly at sundown, the messenger came. "Let us speak first," he said. "We will wrestle and you will conquer me. When I am without life, clean the grass and weeds from a piece of ground and soften the earth. Then take off my clothes and put me in the earth. Cover me. Come often to clear the weeds, but do not disturb the earth. Then wait. I will return to life in a different form."

Again they wrestled. Wunzh felt a new strength and won. Then he did what the messenger had told him.

Many days later, he and his father came to tend the earth. They saw a stem with large green leaves coming through the grave. The stem grew and grew until it was a beautiful plant with gleaming leaves. Then, from one green leaf, grew a fruit shining with silken hair.

"This is the messenger sent by the Great Spirit," said father and son together. "It is Mondahmin. We will learn how to grow this fruit to feed our people."

Then Wunzh went to teach this knowledge to his people. He showed them how to roast the fruit. The Ojibwa ate the fruit and found it sweeter than meat. The fruit was corn, and the corn was Mondahmin.

*Here is a story I heard years ago
from the Algonquin in northern New York State.
They had a good sense of humor and enjoyed
hearing about pranks played on other people.*

Honeyed Words Can't Sweeten Evil

Big Blue Heron was standing in the marsh looking at his reflection in the water. He raised his black-crested head to listen.

Two little White Weasels had come along to the river. They were mother and son. When they saw Blue Heron, they stopped to look.

"What a beautiful big bird-person!" said the son.

"He is called Blue Heron. He carries his head high!"

"Yes, Mother, he is tall as a tree. Were I so tall, I could carry you across this swift river."

Blue Heron was pleased to hear himself so praised. He liked to hear others say that he was big.

He bent down low and spoke to the two. "I will help you go across. Come down to where you see that old tree lying in the stream. I will lie down in the water at the end and put my bill deep into the bank on the other side. You two run across the tree. Then use my body as a bridge and you will get to the other side."

They all went to the old tree lying in the water. Blue Heron lay down in the water at the end and stuck his bill deep into the bank on the other side. Mother and son White Weasel ran lightly and quickly across the log, over Blue Heron, and were safe and dry on the other side. They thanked Blue Heron and said they would tell all the persons in the woods how fine Blue Heron was. Then they went their way.

Old Wolf had been standing on the riverbank watching how the weasels had gotten across.

"What a fine way it would be for me to cross the river. I am old and my bones ache."

When Blue Heron came back to the marsh, Wolf said to him, "Now I know why you Blue Herons are in the marsh — so you can be a bridge for persons to cross the river. I want to go across, but I am old and my bones hurt. Lie down in the water for me so I can cross."

Blue Heron was angry. He didn't like to be called a bridge. Old Wolf saw he had spoken foolish words and decided to use honeyed words.

"You are big and strong, Blue Heron, and that is why your body is such a fine bridge. You could carry me across like a feather."

Blue Heron smiled at Wolf and said, "Old Wolf, get on my back and I'll carry you across."

Wolf grinned from ear to ear thinking how easily he had tricked Blue Heron.

He jumped on the bird's back and Heron went into the rushing river. When he got to the middle, he stopped.

"Friend Wolf," said Blue Heron, "you made a mistake.

I am not strong enough to carry you across. For that you need two herons. I can carry you only halfway. Now you must get another heron to carry you the rest of the way."

He gave his body a strong twist and Wolf fell into the water.

"You wait here, Wolf, for another heron to come and carry you to the other side." Then he flew into the marsh.

The water ran swiftly. No heron came, so where did Wolf go? To the bottom of the river . . .

Since that day, no wolf has ever trusted a heron.

*Ma'nabus is a "folk hero" of the Menominee Indians
in Wisconsin. Many tales are told
about this powerful earth god. He guarded
the Menominee from powers of nature
that would harm them. He taught them how
to make weapons and pottery, and, being very wise,
he directed them to do right. This story tells
how Ma'nabus brought fire to the Menominee
from across Lake Michigan.*

Ma'nabus

Ma'nabus lived with his grandmother, for his mother had died when he was born. One day the two were sitting in the lodge talking. "Grandmother, why haven't we any Fire?"

"Supreme God did not give it to us. Across the Great Lake there is one who has Fire."

"Grandmother, I want to go get it."

"Don't, young one. That old man is very stingy and will never give it to you."

"He will give it to me. Remember, I can call him Grandfather."

"You will throw time away. No begging will get it from that stingy old fellow."

Ma'nabus argued more, but his grandmother said "No!"

At last Ma'nabus said, "I know I can get it and I am

going. You get some kindling wood ready so we can start Fire quickly when I return."

The old grandmother gave up and went with him to the door. Before she could say a word, Ma'nabus had turned himself into a little white rabbit who went hopping out of sight into the green wood.

Ma'nabus loped and hopped along very fast. When he was tired, he changed himself into a fox who was not tired and could run fast. He changed himself many times before he came at last to the Great Lake, where he saw a torn old wigwam.

"I wonder who lives there," he said, changing into his own self. "I'll go and see."

He went in and there in the cold wigwam sat an old woman in thin, torn clothes.

"How goes it, Grandmother?" he said in a friendly voice, and sat down near her.

"Not well. Just look at me, Grandchild. And how goes it with you? From where do you come?"

"It is a long, long tale and I am in a hurry. I am looking for Fire. Do you have any?"

"No, I have not. But across the Great Lake lives an old man who has Fire."

"That must be Grandfather. He will give it to me. Show me the way to him. When I come back with Fire, I will give you some."

The old woman shuffled to the door and pointed the way. "The Fire-keeper lives there."

"Thanks, Grandmother. I will see you when I come back."

Ma'nabus changed himself into a thistledown and commanded a wind to come up. The wind arose and blew him swiftly across the Great Lake, setting him down near the spring of the Fire-keeper. Then Ma'nabus changed into a wet and bedraggled little white rabbit.

The Fire-keeper lived in a big lodge separated into two parts. He stayed on one side, and his two pretty young daughters on the other. The girls were playing on their side of the lodge.

"Sister, go get water," the elder said.

"I'll go," said the younger daughter, and she took a bark bucket and went to the spring. There she came upon a little white rabbit hopping around the spring.

"What a pretty little rabbit," she cried, and she ran after him and soon caught him.

"Sister! Sister," she cried, "I have caught a little white rabbit! I'm bringing him." She quickly filled the bucket with water and ran to the lodge.

Her elder sister met her. "Come let us take him near Fire and warm him."

The father on the other side of the lodge heard their cries and they annoyed him. He shouted, "What are you two making such a fuss about? I have told you to be quiet often enough!"

The girls became very quiet. They warmed the little white creature and soon he was hopping all over. But he was thinking fast, "If that mat which divides the lodge would swing back and forth, Fire would blaze and perhaps I could catch a spark."

Suddenly the mat swung over Fire. Sparks flew up,

and one of them fell on Ma'nabus' back. He jumped up
as if burnt and shot out through the door.

"He is burnt," the girls cried. "Let us catch him."

They ran out looking for him, but the little rabbit
had disappeared into the woods. They looked and called
for him, but he was gone.

"What are you looking for?" their father demanded.

They told him about the little rabbit and the spark
of Fire.

"Ha!" the old man said. "That was Ma'nabus. Long
ago it was told he would get Fire from me, and so it
has happened."

Ma'nabus raced through the fields and woods, with
Fire still on his back, and he came to the Great Lake.

"I want to be a thistledown and want a wind to fly
me across," he said.

As he spoke, so it happened. In no time he was at the

tattered old wigwam where lived the old woman.

"I'll soon be back with your Fire," he shouted, and raced on to his grandmother's lodge.

"Grandmother!" he sang out. "Is your kindling ready? I have Fire. I asked old Grandfather and he gave it to me," he boasted.

Old Grandmother was happy to see him and they lit the kindling with the spark he carried.

"Where shall I put Fire, Grandson?"

"In the middle of the lodge and there it shall always be." Fire blazed up toward the roof.

"I always wanted Fire and warmth," said Ma'nabus. "Friends will come to our lodge when they see Fire. We will not be lonesome."

"I did not think you could get it," his grandmother said.

Ma'nabus liked to boast. "I knew Grandfather would give it to me." Then he sat watching golden warm Fire.

Suddenly he jumped up. "I forgot!" he cried. "I promised Fire to the old woman."

He took some sparks and raced away to the old lady at the Great Lake.

"Here, Grandmother, is Fire that I promised you."

"Thank you, Grandson. May it burn forever for me and others."

"It will burn and it will follow you wherever you camp," said Ma'nabus. "You will not have to build it again. It will always burn."

That's how the Menominee first had Fire. Later, it was different.

*Mosquito stories are famous in our land
and I am sure you know why. Mosquitos have
always been a pesky plague to people.
This tale of Great Father Mosquito is told
by the Tuscarora, who are part of the Iroquois
family. They believed there were two great monster
mosquitos who destroyed many of their people.
One monster was destroyed by Hiawatha. The other
lived on the Seneca River in New York State.*

The Great Father Mosquito

One time there lived a giant Mosquito. He was bigger than a bear and more terrifying. When he flew through the air, the Sun couldn't be seen and it became dark as night. The zooming of his wings was wilder than a storm. And when he was hungry, he would fly into a camp and carry off an Indian or two and pick their bones clean.

Again and again the Tuscarora tried to destroy the wild beast but their arrows fell off him like dew drops off a leaf. They did not know what to do.

So the chief and the medicine men in the tribe ordered a big meeting to pray to the Great Father in Heaven to take pity on them and help them destroy the monster

Mosquito. They burned great fires and they sang, and they danced and they prayed.

The Great Father in Heaven, the Sky Holder, heard their loud cry for help and decided to come to their rescue. He came down from the sky, looking for the monster to do battle with him and destroy him.

The great Mosquito heard this and he knew he could not beat the Sky Holder, so he decided to run away. He flew and he flew and he flew so fast no one could see him. He was faster than lightning. The only sound was the wild zooming of his wings through the air. But Sky Holder was after him just as fast.

The giant monster flew around lakes, over rivers and over mountains toward the East. Sky Holder kept after him, never tiring.

When Sun was going down in a red mist at the end of

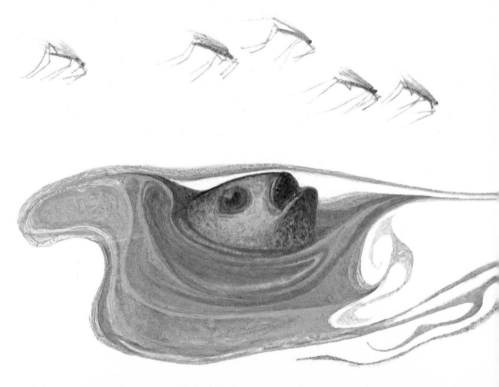

the sky, the great monster came to the large lakes of the East. He turned to look and saw the Great Father was coming nearer.

Swiftly and wildly, at the speed of eagles, the monster flew toward the Salt Lake and there the Sky Holder reached him. The battle was short and the monster Mosquito was destroyed. His blood spattered and flew in all directions. And . . . a strange thing happened. From the blood were born small mosquitos with sharp stingers.

No sooner were they born than they attacked Sky Holder without fear. They stung him so hard he was sorry for what he had done, but he could not undo it. These small mosquitos with the sharp stingers multiplied a thousandfold.

It happened long ago, but to this day we have thousands of mosquitos with sharp stingers.

The elements of heat and cold played
an important part in the lives of most
American Indians. Often their very lives
depended on the weather. This story tells how
the Cherokee felt about cold and heat.

The Sad Marriage of North

North rushed through wide spaces over the waters and lands. He roared and rose, turning and flying from tribe to tribe, through Trees, through Grass, and through Flowers, looking for a wife. He wanted a person to share his travels and to look after his home.

North rushed in gusts and whirls, roaring sometimes in a voice of thunder, sometimes in a voice gentle as Spring.

"I want someone for my shining white home, and I want someone to fly with me over the big spaces."

One day he came where South lived, and there he saw South's beautiful daughter. Her face shone with a glow that lit the world, and her eyes were rays of warmth.

"Will you be my wife?" roared North, as gently as he could. The radiant girl looked at North and bowed her head.

"You must speak to my father," she said.

North blustered and blew, and then spoke to the girl's father.

"No, you cannot have my daughter," the father said. "Go away from here. We don't want you in our land. Since you have come here, it has been cold. I never was so cold before. If you stay longer, we will freeze and die." But North loved South's daughter, and stayed and begged.

"I love your daughter. If you let me marry her, I will take her to my own land that gleams and glitters. It will not be cold here any more."

To save his people the father said, "Yes," and there was a great celebration for the two who were married. Then North took his bride to her new home.

It was a strange land. There were great houses made of glittering cold ice, and people lived in them but they had no fires in them. North brought his bride to his house of hard ice. It was in the evening time. The next morning when his bride of the south arose (she was really Sun), it became warm in the ice house. Warmer and warmer it became, and the ice house began to melt. That had never happened before. People from all around came to see.

Sun began walking through the land of the north and other ice homes began to melt. The houses melted more and more.

"You must send your bride back to her own home. She will destroy our homes and she will destroy us. You cannot have her here," persons were saying.

"I love her and I want her to stay with me. I want her here," the young husband begged. But it was getting

hotter and hotter, and the ice homes were melting quickly.

Everyone was now begging North to send his bride home to her parents. So, in the end, he gave in with a very sad heart. He loved his bride, but he could not have his people destroyed. She was sad, but she understood the trouble of these people, and so went home to her own people.

Since that time, the cold places have stayed cold and the warm places have stayed warm.

*Since bears were common in the northern part
of New York State, where this story comes from,
tales of bears were a normal part
of the story-telling life of the Seneca people.*

The Adventures of the Seneca Chief

One time, many, many years ago, the Senecas were on the warpath, led by their Chief, who was a very wise warrior. They went through weaving summer valleys and they went through woods with high trees. They went through rushing streams and along wide green lakes looking for the enemy.

Suddenly, scouts running in the fore stopped short. There were tracks! Strange tracks! Footmarks of an animal-person they had never seen before! They waited for the Chief and the warriors to come to study the footmarks. All examined them carefully.

Then the Chief, who was a very wise and knowing man, spoke. "They are the tracks of the greatest living Bear in the land. He has no hair, except for one tuft on his back. He is very cunning and very ferocious. That Bear could eat our whole tribe and still eat more. He can smell his prey from far distances and he will be here soon. We must destroy the Bear before he destroys us."

"What can we do?" the warriors asked.

"You stay here. I and the swiftest runner among you will go to battle the Bear. Wait for me here. I am hanging my feather headdress on the limb of this tree. When it falls off, you will know that we have killed the Bear."

The two left, walking through valleys and woods, and came to the place where two big streams joined, making one wide flowing river.

"I think I hear a noise like a great waterfall. Let us stay here," said the Chief.

They stopped and listened. The noise grew louder and louder as if the Thunder God were in the clouds.

"It is Heno, the Thunder God," the warrior said to the Chief.

"No. It is the great hairless Bear, who has smelled us and is coming to attack us. Let us hide quickly behind these great trees."

They hid, and soon the monster Bear was there. He was taller than the giant oak and his skin was bare

except for a thick white tuft on his back. He looked around wildly, scratching the ground and making holes deep enough to hold three men.

The Chief and the warrior began shooting their arrows at the monster. But it was like shooting at solid rock. The Bear's skin was so tough even lightning could not have pierced it. But the arrows made him angry and he began sharpening his claws on the hard stone. He sank his teeth in the giant oak, old as the sun, to sharpen them, splintering the wood far and wide. Then he spied the Seneca Chief, and with fire in his eyes leaped at him.

The Chief was fleet of foot and ran around the thick trunks of the trees, the Bear after him. The monster was gaining ground when the Chief raced to where the rivers met. The Seneca took a giant leap and jumped clear across the running stream.

The Bear could not follow, but now he saw the other Indian. He made a wild leap for him but the warrior raced to the rivers, plunged in, and soon was on the other side.

Seeing the two Indians on the other side of the shore, the Bear decided to go over there too. He tried to leap across and fell into the stream on his back, his paws sticking out of the water.

Now, the monster's heart was in the flesh between his toes, and the wise Seneca Chief knew it.

"Let us shoot our arrows between his toes. That will end him!" the Chief shouted to his companion.

Both sent arrows into his toes. The giant Bear roared like thunder that made the trees and mountains shake.

The water leaped high as if to jump out of its bed. Then
. . . it quieted down . . . the arrows had done their work.

The Chief and the warrior started back at once to
bring the good news to the tribe. On the way they met the
men coming toward them.

"Your headdress fell from the tree so we knew you had
conquered the Bear. That is why we came to meet you."

Then they went to where the monster lay. They
dragged him out of the water and built a great fire to
burn him.

Said the Chief, "The ashes of this Bear are strong
poison, but if you take only a small measure, it will
fulfill any wish you desire. You can wish to be a great

hunter, or a great runner, or a great swimmer, or anything."

Each Indian took some of the ashes and made his wish, and the Seneca Chief wished to be the fleetest runner in the tribe.

To each one his wish was granted, and they set out on the warpath in high spirits. Soon they saw an enemy tribe in a green hollow, dancing and drumming.

"I alone will attack them," the Seneca Chief said proudly. "If I could destroy the great monster Bear, I can destroy this enemy."

So the Chief came among the dancers and battled them. At first he was successful, but soon he saw there were too many of them and he tried to flee to his tribe. But they caught him before he could start, and made him prisoner.

"We must punish him for making war on us," said one.

"Since he says he is the fleetest runner in the land, let us burn the soles of his feet."

They did it and filled the blisters with ashes.

"Now show us what a great runner you are. You must race against our fleetest man, and if you don't beat him, you will never run again."

The race was set in a broad valley full of flowers. All the Indians gathered to watch.

The two men were off on the signal. And though his feet were all blisters and he was in great pain, the Seneca Chief still could run as fast as the wind because he had eaten a little of the ashes of the great Bear.

He left the other Indian far behind and was soon out of sight. When he knew he was safe he rested, and at night he climbed a high tree to sleep.

The golden sun came early over the greenwood, bringing good warmth. Suddenly, in the singing of the birds, the Seneca heard a strange voice croaking.

"You are sick and in pain."

"Yes, I am," replied the Chief.

"I knew it and that is why I came here to help you."

The Seneca climbed painfully down the tree and looked around him to see who spoke. He beheld a strange person hopping among the dead leaves, picking herbs from the earth and then crushing the leaves.

"Come, let me rub this on the soles of your feet." And, amazingly, as soon as the herbs touched the flesh, the pain vanished.

"Why do you help me? And who are you?" asked the Seneca Chief.

"You have helped me and my people many times, and when I learned you were in trouble, I came to help you."

"Who are you?" the Chief said again.

"I am the Father of the Toads," the strange person croaked. "Do your feet feel better?"

"Yes, thank you," the Chief said.

"Don't forget me and my people when you return to your home. Help us as you always have."

The Chief swore he would do so and went on his way. Since then Toads and the Senecas have been good friends and have always helped each other in need.

This is a well-known story of Indian heroism told by many tribes. Some say it happened in the old days in what is now Mississippi. This version was told by the Biloxi Indians in Alabama.

The Song That Comes from the Sea

The Biloxi were a great tribe, living in peace and pursuing their work without wars. They tilled the land, hunted, and were good craftsmen.

The tribes around them were not so peaceful. They were often on the warpath to conquer and destroy. Of them all, the Choctaw were the most warlike. They roamed far and wide, through the plains and woods and swamps, fighting successfully all those who crossed their path.

One day a council of Choctaw chiefs decided to go on the warpath against the Biloxi. Although they were not afraid, the Biloxi did not wish war. When they heard the news, they decided to defend their homes and land.

The Choctaw were a big tribe and a fierce one. Soon they were defeating the Biloxi. The Biloxi kept on retreating and retreating until they came to

Pascagoula Bay, which runs out into the wide green sea. Then there was no further retreat except into the green moving waters. So the Biloxi built a fort at the water's edge and entrenched themselves behind it, holding off the enemy as best they could.

Days went by in fierce battle. Soon the fight became more desperate, for now the Biloxi had to battle another enemy — hunger. They could not hunt and their supplies were running low.

One day the Biloxi chiefs met in a war council. They were completely surrounded by the enemy and their food was almost gone. Surrender? If they did, it was certain death to the warriors and fierce violence to the rest.

The old chiefs, their faces calm as shadows, spoke long in voices of rolling clouds. The young warriors, eyes flashing, spoke long and with tongues as biting as sharp winds. All saw but one way out. The sea! They must go all together into the green world of the sea. There the Choctaw could not attack them. There they would have no fear of hunger or violence. There they would have peace.

All solemnly agreed and they set the time for the desperate adventure. The Chief would open the gate that faced the ever-moving sea.

The day came. The sun shone brightly. The wind whispered encouraging words. The rim of the sea was in a golden glow.

The Chief opened the gate and went out, followed by the councilors, heads proudly high, chanting the song of the end. The young warriors followed, looking straight and fearless before them, chanting with the Chief in defiant rhythm.

Then came the women and the young — all, all chanting bravely, almost in voices of rejoicing, like the morning wind in the sunshine. They all walked as if going to a feast, singing and chanting the song of the end.

The first to enter the rainbow spray, the white waves from the far deep-green-without-end, was the Chief. His councilors followed him, and they walked into the sea until the waters quelled their chanting and covered their heads.

Then came the young men, bows and arrows in their hands, singing and chanting of their fearless deeds and of life everlasting. Their song ended when the pearly water covered their heads.

The women and young followed, brave, fearless, and straight as pines. They walked slowly, chanting, daring — straight into the gently-swaying green water. They walked into the waves till the green billows covered their black hair.

So the brave Biloxi showed the fierce Choctaw how men and women could go from the world without fear if they had to.

People say that when the sun rises in the sea over Pascagoula Bay and when it goes down over the green trees on the shore, you can hear the chanting of the death song of these fearless Indians, living peacefully now in the bottom of Pascagoula Bay.

While I was collecting stories
of the Great Lakes states, I visited
some Quapaw Indians near Green Bay.
On a starry evening when we were
swapping tales, I heard this one.

The Cranes of the Great Lakes

One day when the wide world was very young, the Great Spirit said to two Cranes, "You two go down to the earth below the clouds and look through the land. Look until you come to a place where you would like to live. There fold your wings tightly to your sides and stand and wait. Then something wonderful will happen to you. A great change will come over you."

They thanked the Great Spirit and began flying and looking to see how they would come to the earth. When they saw an opening between the clouds, they flew through and went winging downward.

When they came down low, they looked to see where it would be best for them to live.

There was a prairie so big you could not see the end.

"Let us live here," said one Crane. "It is all green and there are flowers. There are also many animals. It is a good place."

"Yes, let us stop here and see if we like it." So they settled in the prairie. They went hunting and ate buffalo meat and it was good. But many times there were no buffalo and they had no food.

"Let us go into the forest. There we can get food easier. Maybe we should live there."

So they went into the woods and hunted elk and deer and other animals. But hunting was not easy and often they could not find elk or deer.

"We must find another place where hunting is easier."

They flew everywhere looking until one day they came to the Great Lakes. The lakes were so big that sometimes you could not see from one shore to the other. The lakes were full of fish to eat.

There was no end of fish in the lakes, in the rapids, and in the inlets. There were more fish than anyone could want.

"Let us try to live here," they said. And they found a place and every day they flew over the lakes, over the rapids and the inlets. Wherever they flew there was always plenty of fish. And it was much easier than hunting.

"Here it is good to live," they said.

After a time they remembered the words of the Great Spirit. They flew to a hill that was near the water and there they stopped at the highest place.

They folded their wings tightly against the sides of their bodies as they had been told to do and stood still. Then the Great Spirit looked down at them and saw their faith in him.

Slowly a great change came over them and . . . they became a man and a woman. They were the first man and woman there. And they were the first man and woman of the Crane Indian tribe in that part of the land.

*The Penobscot Indians living
by the Penobscot River on the land
now called Maine had a great folk hero.
His name was Gluska'be, and he was a trickster
and a magician who used his arts to help
his people. The tales of this hero show how
the Indians looked upon the creation of nature.
Here I tell of three of Gluska'be's deeds
that made life better for the
Penobscot Indians.*

Gluska'be,
the Penobscot Hero

Gluska'be lived with his Grandmother Woodchuck, who taught him hunting, fishing, and weaving.

When he was grown up he said to his grandmother, "Make me a bow and arrows. I am tired of eating rabbit which you give me. Now I will bring the food."

She made him a bow and arrows, and he went into the woods and brought back deer and bear. His grandmother was proud of him and she sang and she danced. "We will have plenty of meat and fat," she sang.

"Now show me how to make a canoe, Grandmother. I want to go duck hunting." She showed him, but when he went hunting in his canoe a wild Wind was rushing over the water and he could not get any ducks. He came home, broke off a few rocks, and made a stone canoe. But that was no better — the wild Wind knocked it around like a feather.

So Gluska'be went back to the wigwam and said, "Grandmother, wild Wind overturned my canoe and if he can do that, he must be able to do harm to the Indian people. Tell me where the great Wind lives. I must stop the great blowing."

"He lives very far away, Grandson."

"Not too far for me. I am going and I'll be back soon."

She told him the way, and Gluska'be walked and walked and walked. The nearer he came to Wind, the fiercer Wind blew. On the seventh day Wind blew so fiercely he took all the hair from Gluska'be's head.

Suddenly Gluska'be saw a giant Bird waving great, heavy wings. These wings were making the wild Wind. Gluska'be walked slowly to the Bird, the Wind Maker.

"Grandfather," he said, "you could make greater waves in the air if you were up on the mountain. Why not go there?"

"That is true, Grandson without hair, but I must stay here where I have been since the beginning, because I can't reach the mountain."

"I will help you get there, Grandfather."

"I will be happy if you do."

Gluska'be picked up the giant Bird and began to climb the mountain. When he got halfway he dropped the Bird as if by accident, and one of his wings broke.

Gluska'be looked sad. "Now you must stay here, Grandfather, and make Wind blow with only one wing. I must go. I hope your wing will heal." But in his head, Gluska'be was glad. "It will be calm," he said to himself. "My people and I can now go duck hunting."

Gluska'be took his canoe on the lake to hunt, but the water was calm for so long that the weeds and the grass in it became too thick for a canoe to glide through.

"This is not good, there must be a little Wind. I will go back to Wind Maker."

He went back, but Wind Maker did not recognize him, for his hair had grown back.

The Bird was sitting alone, sad and silent. He could not move.

"Grandfather, I will heal your wing and take you to the place where you sat before. Then you can blow as you used to."

"Grandson, I will rejoice if you do this."

"But you must promise you will not make a great Wind all the time," said Gluska'be. "Beat your wings softly sometimes and sometimes rest."

"I will do that, Grandson. Before, Wind was too strong all the time."

Gluska'be healed the wing and put the Bird back where he was before. Then he went home. And from then on it happened as Wind Maker had promised.

And then . . .

There was a long and bitter cold where Gluska'be and his people lived.

"Grandmother," said Gluska'be, "Winter Cold is too long and brings misery to Indians. I must bring Summer. Where does he live?"

"Summer lives in the South and is guarded day and night."

"I am going there. Make a pair of snowshoes. Then cut hide strips and make me seven big balls from them."

She did as he asked, and he went away. Soon he could not use his snowshoes for it was too warm. So he hung them on a tall tree, and told a cicada to watch them.

He walked on until he came to a wigwam where people were dancing.

"Why are you dancing?" he asked.

"Why are you asking?" they answered gruffly.

Gluska'be laughed and turned their noses upside down.

He watched the dancers make turns and swirl around a great bowl. Inside it was a yellow-golden jelly which was Summer.

Two young girls danced near him.

"Why are you dancing, pretty girls?" he asked.

They made faces at him mockingly.

So he gently stroked their backs with his magic hands. Slowly they changed into toads and sat down. The other dancers kept on turning.

"I must get Summer from them," Gluska'be said softly.

He made the wigwam dark, took the great bowl with Summer in it, and ran out.

As the wigwam became light again, the dancers saw that the bowl with Summer was gone.

"Summer has been taken by the stranger!" they cried, and ran out to search for him.

They became giant crows and flew in all directions. Soon they saw Gluska'be and swooped down on him.

He had put a ball of hide strips on his head. The crows took hold of it, thinking it was Gluska'be's head, but soon they saw that it was not. They flew back to him and swooped down, but again he had put a ball of hide strips on his head. The giant crows picked it off only to find again that it was not his head.

They did this five more times, then became tired and did not follow him any more.

Gluska'be ran until he came to the tree where his snowshoes were. He put them on and raced to the great Ice House where the giant Ice sat all the time breathing icy air into the land.

"What do you want, Grandson?" he said.

"You must end blowing your ice-cold air all the time, for it makes people suffer."

"They can look at my starry ice."

"Cold all the time brings suffering. I will end it."

"You are not strong enough."

"No, but I brought one with me who is." He put Summer before him, and the great Ice-person began to melt and drip.

"Take him away!" he roared. "Grandson, you are killing me!" His nose had melted away.

"It is too cold, and persons suffer too much," said Gluska'be.

"Take him away!"

Chief Ice-person's arms and legs melted. Then his great body grew smaller and smaller.

"Take . . . take. . . ." He was all melted, and could say no more.

Gluska'be was satisfied. "Now it won't be so cold and fierce. Summer, you stay here. When you are tired go away so that Ice-person can bring Winter back. But after a time you must come back so people can have a rest from Ice-person's Winter Cold."

And so it was.

And then . . .

Gluska'be walked along the paths of his people. One day he came to a place where the Indians were weak and sad.

"Why do you look so weak? Why do you look so sad?"

"We have no water. A monster Frog, Water Guard, sits on the river holding water back from us. He is killing us."

"I will make him give you water," Gluska'be said.

So the people followed Gluska'be to the place where the monster Frog, Water Guard, was holding back the water.

"Why do you let my grandchildren die? Why do you keep water from them? You will be punished for being so cruel. Water should be shared. Now I will give them water."

He got hold of monster Frog, and there was a great fight. Gluska'be broke the Frog's neck, but that did not seem to hurt him. He still held on to the water.

Gluska'be then got his ax and cut down a giant yellow birch. He cut it in such a way that it fell on monster Frog and killed him.

The water began gushing and flowing, and as it traveled, it made the Penobscot River.

The Indians were so thirsty they jumped into the river and drank and drank, but they did not know the water had magic, and some of them turned into Fish, some into Turtles, and some into Frogs.

There were a few who escaped and remained persons, and they and their children lived along the Penobscot River and took its name for their own.

*Stories of animals changing into people
and people changing into animals are told
everywhere in the world.
In this Labrador tale, Fox Woman helps
a lonely hunter, until he tries to solve
the mystery of her appearance.*

The Eskimo Indian and His Fox Wife

Far up in the cold North, where winds blow sharply and snow falls thickly, an Indian hunter lived all alone. His only friends were Sun, Wind, Snow, and Stars.

When he got up in the morning, he had to prepare his own food and clean his house. When he came home, he had to scrape his own skin-clothing and his skin-boots and hang them out to dry. And he had to do his own cooking and washing. It was not an easy life for him.

One day, when daylight was sinking into darkness, he came home and stopped at his door. To his great surprise, everything was in order as it had never been before. The earthen floor was swept and the food in the pot was steaming hot and ready to eat. Everything was in order as if a good wife had done it.

Who *had* done it? He looked all over — everywhere — inside and outside. There was no one around. He ate the good food and lay down to sleep, wondering who had done this good deed for him.

The next morning he went out to hunt as he always did, and when he came home . . . he found his home all in fine order again, and his food was ready for him — just as the day before! His skin-clothing was scraped and his boots were hanging up to dry. Again he looked and looked to find who was so kind to him, but he couldn't find tracks anywhere. He just couldn't understand it.

Day after day the hunter found his house and clothes cared for. Then he said to himself, "I must find out who does all these things for me. Only a good wife would do it and I have no wife. Who can it be? I must find the person."

Next morning he went out hunting as he always did, but he only went a little distance and then turned back and hid near the house to watch.

Pretty soon a sleek fox with a long red tail came loping along. It ran right up to the house and went in.

"That fox is going into my house to steal my food," the Indian said to himself.

He crept up to his house and looked in, ready to slay the fox. But when he saw what was there, he stopped in great surprise.

Right in the middle of the room there was a beautiful girl, dressed in the finest skin-clothes he had ever seen. And on the wall he saw hanging . . . the skin of a fox!

"Who are you?" the Indian cried. "What are you doing here? Why do you clean my house? Did you cook my food? Is it you who cleaned my skins and boots?"

"Yes, I have cleaned this house and cooked your food. I have scraped these skins and dried your boots. I have done what I do well," the beautiful girl said. "Now you see how life can be made easier. I hope you are pleased. I do what I can do well. Then I feel happy and proud."

"I am pleased," said the hunter. "Will you stay with me all the time? I would be proud to share this life and my home with you. Then I too could do what I do well."

"Very well, I will stay. But you must promise never to complain about me, or to ask from where I came."

The hunter promised. From then on, they were happy to be together as husband and wife. He did the hunting while she prepared the skins and took care of their home.

Everything was fine. They were good and hard workers.

One day, the man smelled a strange, musky odor that he did not like.

"Woman," the man said, "there is a strange, musky odor in the house since you have come here. You must have brought it with you."

"Yes, it came with me, and it is a good smell."

"Where have you brought it from?" asked the hunter.

"You have broken the promises you made! You said you would not complain about me. And you promised not to ask from where I came. Now I must leave you."

The woman threw away her skin-dress and put on her fox skin that had been hanging on the wall. Then she slipped out of the house as a fox.

From that time on, the man lived alone. He had to do everything himself, just as before the Fox Woman had come to him. And she never returned.

Of all the Indians in North America
perhaps the Zuñi of the Southwest have created
the finest poetry. This poetic spirit enters
their daily lives, their songs, their dances,
their festivals, and their faith.
This story is one fragment from the rich
tapestry of tales in the Zuñi creation cycle.

In the Beginning

First there was only darkness over everything. It filled all Space. It covered the whole world.

The ancient Sun Father, dwelling in the Great Outer Spaces, gazed around with his all-seeing eyes and saw that all was covered with water. Wherever he looked, there was only water.

He wanted life to come on the water. So he rubbed his hands together, and from the skin that came off, he made two great balls. Raising his hand high, he threw one of the balls on the surface of the water. The ball melted slowly and spread all over the great waters. It spread far and wide and grew bigger and bigger. As it grew, part of it sank into the water.

Then he threw the second ball from his hand into the water. That too spread all over, growing even larger than the first. It drew up all the water that was left by the first ball.

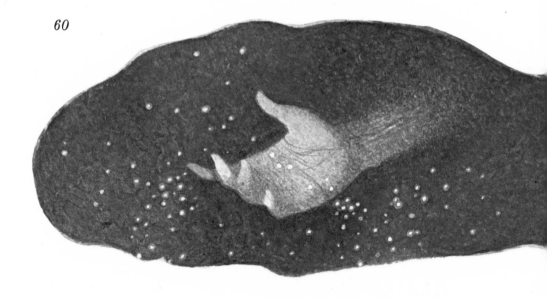

Time went on and the first ball became Mother Earth and the second became Father Sky.

So there was water on Mother Earth and water in Father Sky. And that is why Father Sky is blue.

Mother Earth gave birth to man and creatures. One day Mother Earth and Father Sky held a great council.

"How will our children live?" said Mother Earth. "We must have food for our children. How, after they are born, shall they live and be guided?"

"They will be guided by my hands when I am not near.

"Behold!" said Father Sky, and he spread out his great hands palm downward. There was yellow corn in every line and wrinkle of his palms and fingers.

"The shining kernels will tell them what to do and how to live. They will be their guiding stars."

When you look into the sky at night, you see the palms of Father Sky and in them the gleaming stars to guide his children.

Said Mother Earth, "They still need more guidance to walk over the world."

She poured water into an earthen bowl, put saliva in it and whipped it swiftly around with her fingers. Soon there was foam rising high above the rim of the bowl.

Then Mother Earth blew on the foam and flake after flake broke off and flew all over, bursting all around.

Said Mother Earth, "White foam-clouds like this will rise and burst to give them water to drink and water to help them grow food to eat and live. The features of my face will form the mountains of the land and to these the people will give names. These will guide them in going from place to place.

"At night when your corn-star-fingers watch over them and they are cold, my children will rest in my bosom and will find warmth and strength to live from one day to another."

That, say the Zuñi Indians, was In the Beginning.

This Texas Indian tale is probably based
on a natural catastrophe of long ago.
Tales such as this grow in the telling
from generation to generation, and reflect
an artistic-religious inventiveness.

The Enchanted Mountain

Once many years ago there was a beautiful rich valley in the northern part of Texas. There were palms full of dates reaching to the heavens; there was no end of green trees. And there was a wonderful big lake. It was so big that you could not see the end or the other side of it. The lake was full of fish and it gave good food to the Indian tribe living nearby.

The Indians said that there lived in that lake a fierce Evil Spirit, and a kind Good Spirit. The Good Spirit held down the Evil Spirit who wanted to destroy the land and the people. He watched that Evil Spirit all the time so that he could not carry out his terrible threat.

No Indian was permitted to touch the water of the lake during a feast or ceremony. If it was touched, the Evil Spirit would escape and destroy the village and the Indians by sinking them into the water. No Indian had ever disobeyed the order. They lived in peace. There was plenty of hunting and good fishing.

The Chief of the Indians who lived on that lake had a

beautiful daughter with black eyes and long black hair. One young warrior of the tribe loved her, and she loved him, but her father had different plans. He had promised her to the chief of the neighboring tribe and a daughter had to obey.

The day of the marriage was set and the two tribes decided to first go on a great hunt so there would be plenty of food for everyone. All the braves of both tribes went, except the young Indian who loved the Chief's daughter.

The young bride and her lover were in deep sorrow. In the evening they came to the lake, sitting close to one another and saying little. Then the girl went home, but the brave stayed on, looking at the great lake and at the endless stars in the sky.

For a long time he sat looking at the water and suddenly he saw on it a big canoe paddled by a giant Indian. It came right up to the shore where he was sitting, and the big Indian jumped out and came to him.

"You sit and grieve because the one you love will be taken from you tomorrow," he said. "But it need not be. I have come to help you."

"Who are you?"

"I said, I have come to help you."

"How can you help me?"

"Tomorrow when they have the feast and the dancing for the marriage, I will come in my canoe. When I come to the shore, you will bring the girl into the canoe and I will take you where you will be safe. I will take you where no one can follow."

"The wise men say no one must touch the water during a feast or ceremony."

"Don't be afraid. You will both leap into the canoe and will not touch the water."

Then the giant Indian went off in his canoe. It was the Evil Spirit of the lake who had escaped for a time and had come to tempt the young warrior.

The night of the great feast came — when the bride was to marry the chief whom she had never seen. Big fires burned under the palms near the shore of the lake. The wigwams were decorated with flowers. The game from the great hunt was on the fire, and all were in a festive mood and ready for the wedding.

The bride was dressed in beautiful skins ornamented with feathers and stones. Suddenly there was a black

spot on the waters of the lake. All were frightened. What did it mean? It was the time when none could touch the water.

The black spot became a canoe. It came nearer and all saw a giant Indian holding the paddle. He was now right at the shore. As the canoe touched the ground, the young Indian picked up the bride in his arms and swiftly ran to the beach. But he touched the water as he leaped into the canoe!

The boat shot out like an arrow and none tried to stop it. All were afraid to touch the water.

Now from out of the calm came a great roar and the water rose wildly, mountain high. Lightning raged through the sky. Then with a great crash, the earth tore apart and masses of rocks rose high, becoming great mountains. The water raised the canoe like a feather, but

in it were only the young Indian and his love. The giant Evil Spirit had disappeared.

All the scene had changed. Where there once were palms and other trees, there were now masses of granite. The lake was not there; it was swallowed into the earth. There were stones and rocks all over. And up had come a granite mountain. On the top of it were great boulders and rocks that looked like a canoe with two Indians sitting in it. The two lovers!

The Enchanted Mountain! No lake. Only a spring whose waters ran down the Enchanted Stone Mountain like a silver thread.

All had changed. The Indian tribe was no more. It had been swallowed by the earth like the lake and the trees. Just a few Indians were left who led a poor life amidst the mountain rocks.

*This is the kind of story the Sia Indians
liked to tell at night around the fire
when they wanted a good laugh.*

How Rabbit Got the Best of Coyote

One sunny day Coyote was running through the hills. Suddenly he saw Rabbit sitting before his house.

"Ha! I'll catch you," he thought. "I'll have a fine dinner." He leaped on him and caught him between his teeth.

"Man-Coyote, Man-Coyote! Don't eat me!" Rabbit cried. "Don't eat me. Wait! I'll tell you something that is of great importance and you'll be glad to hear it."

Coyote was curious. "Let me hear it."

"I must sit in front of my door to tell it the right way," said Rabbit. "Here I am too cold. At the door I can tell it better."

"I'll let you go to your door, but I'll stand near to watch."

Rabbit went to the door of his house, sat down, and said, "What are you thinking, Coyote?"

"Nothing," he answered.

"Then hear me. I am Rabbit. I am afraid of people. I am most afraid when they come with bows and arrows. Then I tremble and shake like a leaf in the wind."

Rabbit began trembling like a sapling in March.

When Coyote saw it, he was much surprised. He had never seen that before and he couldn't understand it. He shook his head, and the minute he wasn't looking, Rabbit ran away swiftly.

Coyote ran after him, but he couldn't run as fast and couldn't catch him.

Rabbit came to his friend's house and ran in. Coyote came up quickly.

"This is a stone house," he said, "but I am hungry and I'll get that Rabbit and teach him a lesson." He butted his head against the door. He pulled the stones. But no matter how hard he tried the stones would not crumble.

"I'll get Rabbit," cried Coyote, wild with anger. Rabbit, inside, heard him and began mocking him.

"How will you get me, Coyote? The stones will break your teeth."

"I'll get you, and you won't get away this time! I can't break the stones but I can kill you with fire."

"Ha! There is no wood here!"

"Then I'll burn grass. I will burn it by the door and smoke will go into your eyes and nose and will kill you."

"Fine! My food will not kill me. Grass is my friend."

"Then I'll bring the trees from the woods and set them on fire before your door."

"All the trees know me. They are my friends too. They won't do me any harm."

"Well, then, I'll get the gum from the piñon trees to burn everything in your house. The fire will go into your eyes and face and burn you."

"Oh," cried Rabbit, "the gum from the piñon trees is not my friend. I am afraid."

"Ah! Now I know how to finish you and eat you roasted."

Coyote ran out and picked all the gum he could find on the piñons and brought it to the door of the house where Rabbit was. When he had a big heap, he set fire to it.

"Now, Rabbit inside, you'll have to come out or roast."

"The smoke is coming in. The fire is coming in. It's going in my eyes," Rabbit cried.

"Watch me help Fire." Coyote went near to the fire and blew on it to make it burn better.

"Oh, I am burning," Rabbit cried.

Coyote laughed and went nearer to the flames.

"I'll help you, Rabbit," he said. "I'll blow the flames so they become strong." He went still nearer to the flames to blow with all his strength.

"Oh," cried Rabbit, "your mouth is so close to the fire you are blowing it into my eyes and my mouth. Don't blow so hard. Don't!"

Coyote did the opposite. He came nearer and nearer, right up to the flames, and blew harder.

Rabbit had been watching all the time to make sure Coyote was near enough to the fire, then . . . he gave a great push to the burning gum. It flew into Coyote's face and eyes and nose, burning him and blinding him. He fell on the ground, rolling all over with pain.

Out leaped Rabbit and ran off swiftly. Coyote did not follow him. He was too busy trying to get the gum out of his eyes and nose. He forgot all about Rabbit.

Great herds of buffalo once roamed
the plains where the grass grew thick.
The Comanche Indians hunted the buffalo for food,
clothing, and shelter. As you might expect,
there were often great tales of the buffalo.

In the Days
of the Great Buffalo

Once there came a summer when Rain forgot the plains. Streams were dry and showed only white stone beds. The grass withered and from the heavens came only streams of heat. All the green was scorched.

The Comanche moved from place to place, but they found no water and no buffalo. The great dryness had driven all animals to other lands. There was nothing to eat and no water to drink. Women and children and old men were too weak to walk. The hunters sat, bows and arrows in hand. There was no shade in which to rest.

The saddest of all was their great Chief. The sight of his suffering people was to him worse than his own hunger and thirst.

He went away from his tepees to be alone and to pray. He prayed long to the Great Spirit to bring life-giving Rain and to send the buffalo once again to the plains so that his people would not starve. Then he rose from his prayer and went back to his tribe.

Said he to the warriors and councilors, "I have prayed to the Great Spirit to help us and now I will go out to hunt. In six days I will come back with food for you."

He walked out on the dry plain toward the rising Sun. For two days he traveled on the brown grass under the heat of the bleaching Sun. But he found no water and no buffalo. He was swaying from side to side, nearly ready to fall from hunger and thirst, when suddenly he stopped. He was not sure of what he saw. It looked green. He was afraid to trust his eyes, but he dragged himself slowly to it. Yes, it was green. A grove of green trees unscorched by the Sun. And in that green grove there was water!

Seeing the green and the water gave him joy and

strength. First he drank long and deep. Then he looked around. There at the water's edge were the tracks of buffalo. Tracks of a giant herd. Young ones, old ones. And the trail was fresh!

"The Great Spirit heard my prayers for my people. He is good to us. I will follow the tracks of this herd."

He rested, and then full of strength he followed the tracks, looking sharply about him all the time.

Suddenly he saw in the distance something as big as a mountain. "I wonder what it is. There are no mountains on these plains. And it seems to be moving. Mountains don't move!"

He went nearer, his eyes on the great moving thing. He was a little afraid, and when he came close he was terrified.

It was a giant buffalo, big as a mountain. He had never seen such a buffalo before. It had a thousand feet.

"These must have made the buffalo tracks I saw at the water," thought the Chief.

The giant head of the buffalo turned toward him. The Chief's heart was weak with fear.

A sound came through the air. A voice. It came from afar on the hot wind.

"Don't be afraid. You can slay the buffalo. He cannot do you any harm and he will give food to your tribe. Don't be afraid!"

The Chief raised his bow and aimed his arrow straight and strong. Again and again he drew his arrows to his breast, shooting with all his strength.

The great, giant buffalo fell to the ground with a thundering noise. The earth shook and a deep cleft opened.

The Chief took some meat from the hump, made a fire, roasted and ate it. Then he cut a great chunk of meat and put it on his back to bring to his people.

He walked toward the setting Sun. When he had traveled some distance from the fresh water and green trees, he saw his people coming to meet him. They were walking slowly.

"Why are you walking on the road?" the Chief asked.

"We were waiting for you as you told us. Then a voice came from the winds. The voice told us to go to meet you, that you would give us food and drink. That is why we are here."

"The Great Spirit watches over us and is helping us. Come, I will lead you to the place where there is water for all, and good meat for all."

They followed him to the water. They drank and drank until they had enough. Then the Chief led them to the place where the great buffalo lay, and all ate until their hunger was gone and they were again strong in body.

From the hide of the great buffalo they made shields to protect themselves against the enemy. No arrows could pierce that hide, so the Comanche tribe could not be conquered by any enemy.

That is why the Comanche still remember and like to tell the tale of the Days of the Great Buffalo.

The Ute Indians lived in the territory
we call Utah and Colorado. To them, the first gods
in the world were animal-persons
who had human traits and supernatural gifts.
This story tells you how they believed
their animal-god-persons acted in this world.

Kwi-na the Eagle

I'-o-wi, the soft Turtle Dove, with her child strapped tightly on her back, walked along the field gathering seeds. It was not easy work and she was tired. So she sat under the Sage bush, where her little sister O-ho-tcu, the Summer Yellow Bird, was playing.

"O-ho-tcu," she said, "play with my son under the Sage bush and watch him. Work will be easier for me." Then I'-o-wi went back to her task.

Tso-a-vwits the Witch, who was nearby, rushed up. When O-ho-tcu saw her, she was scared because she knew that witches steal boys and not girls.

Said the Witch, "Is this your little brother?"

"No, it's my little sister." But the Witch knew the child was the son of O-ho-tcu's sister. She changed herself into a frightful person with fangs and wild hair and screamed, "O-ho-tcu, little girls should tell the truth!"

Summer Yellow Bird was so frightened she could not shout or move.

The Witch picked up the little boy and ran away with him to her lodge. There she laid him down, took hold of one of his legs and pulled it and stretched it until it was as large as a man's. Then she did the same to the other leg and also to his arms and body until he was as big as a Ute warrior.

Although he had the body of a man, he had the mind of a child. When the Witch said "Marry me," the boy obeyed and became her husband, U-ja the Sage Cock.

When I'-o-wi, his mother, came back, she found her son gone, and O-ho-tcu crying.

"Why do you cry? Where is my son?"

O-ho-tcu told how Tso-a-vwits had run away with him.

The mother was very angry and scolded her and punished her. "I must find my son," she cried, and she ran off to look for him.

I'-o-wi looked and looked but did not find him. Her friends came to help her and so did her brother, Kwi-na the Eagle.

Kwi-na traveled high, looking everywhere. One day he heard a strange sound. Following it, Kwi-na found Tso-a-vwits the Witch and her husband, U-ja the Sage Cock. But Kwi-na did not know that the boy-man was his sister's child.

Swiftly he came back to his sister and told her that he had seen the Witch and her husband, U-ja.

"It must be my son," I'-o-wi cried. "Tso-a-vwits has bewitched him and made him into a man. I must go to him. If he hears me crying and calling him, he will know that I am his mother. Then he will come to me. Take me to them."

Kwi-na the Eagle placed his sister on his wide wings and took her to the lodge of the Witch. I'-o-wi climbed a tall cedar tree nearby and began weeping and calling to her son. Kwi-na sat in a nearby tree and waited to see what would happen.

When U-ja heard his mother's voice, he remembered everything. "I hear my mother! I hear my mother!" he cried.

Tso-a-vwits said slyly to U-ja, "That is not your mother's voice; it is the voice of a witch wanting to separate us. Come, husband, let us go away from here."

She took U-ja by the hand and led him behind the lodge where lay the skin of a giant mountain sheep U-ja had hunted down. The Witch picked up the dried skin and covered herself and her husband with it.

"Here I'-o-wi will never find us," she mumbled.

The Witch was right. I'-o-wi and all her friends looked and looked and couldn't find the two. But her brother Kwi-na had the wisdom of the sky, and so he said, "They must be hidden under the ground or behind the rocks. Wherever they are hiding, they must come out when they are hungry. I will get a rabbit and put the meat on top of a high pine."

He did as he said he would. Then he peeled the bark of the tree so that it was smooth and hard to climb.

"Now, sister, we will hide and watch. When they come for the meat, Tso-a-vwits will try to climb the tree but she will always slide down. While she is busy climbing and sliding, I will steal your son away from her."

They hid near the peeled pine tree and waited.

The Witch was hungry and her child-husband cried for food. So the two came out of their hiding place looking for something to eat. The Witch quickly smelled the meat on the tree. So did U-ja.

"I'll get the meat," the Witch said.

Again and again she tried to climb up the tree, but each time she slid down.

While she was busy, Kwi-na the Eagle swooped down swiftly and picked up U-ja. He brought him to a place under the Sage bush from which Tso-a-vwits the Witch had taken him. The magic of the Sage bush turned U-ja back into a child, and his mother was happy again.

"The Witch will look for your son," Kwi-na said. "We must hide our tracks."

He flew up into the sky and brought down a fierce storm that made the wind blow wild. Thick rain beat the ground and the tracks were washed away.

Tso-a-vwits the Witch ran through the forest, over the rocks and down into the valleys trying to find the tracks. She saw none, but way under some leaves were eagle feathers, and then she knew.

"It was Kwi-na, the brother of I'-o-wi, who carried my husband away. He is a terrible warrior and I cannot battle him. I will go to To-go'-a the Father Rattlesnake. He will help me and protect me and kill my enemies."

To-go'-a was sleeping on the warm rocks when the Witch came to him. "Grandfather! Grandfather!" she cried.

He awoke and when he saw who it was, he rattled his rattles and shouted, "Go away from here. I want to sleep."

"You must help me, Grandfather. Kwi-na stole my husband. I am afraid of the Eagle-warrior."

Just then they heard Kwi-na screaming.

"Hide me! Hide me, Grandfather! He will kill me," the Witch cried.

"I don't know where to hide you. There is no place here."

"Let me crawl into your mouth!"

To-go'-a opened his mouth wide and the Witch crept in, but she was still scared so she crept into his stomach.

Kwi-na looked and looked.

The Witch was too big for Rattlesnake's stomach and he was in great pain. He told her to get out but she wouldn't. The pain was getting worse. It became so bad that Rattlesnake crawled out of his skin leaving the Witch inside it. She rolled around in it until she got behind the rocks where no one could find her.

"Old Witch, where are you?" Kwi-na was shouting and looking everywhere. "Come out so I can kill you."

Safely hidden, the Witch laughed and mocked him by repeating his last three words. Whatever Kwi-na said, she repeated the last three words. So he flew away.

Ever since, witches have lived in snakes' skins hidden between rocks and they always repeat the last three words they hear.

We may call it Echo but the Indians know better. They know the old tales and know the sound is the voice of witches hidden in snakes' skins.

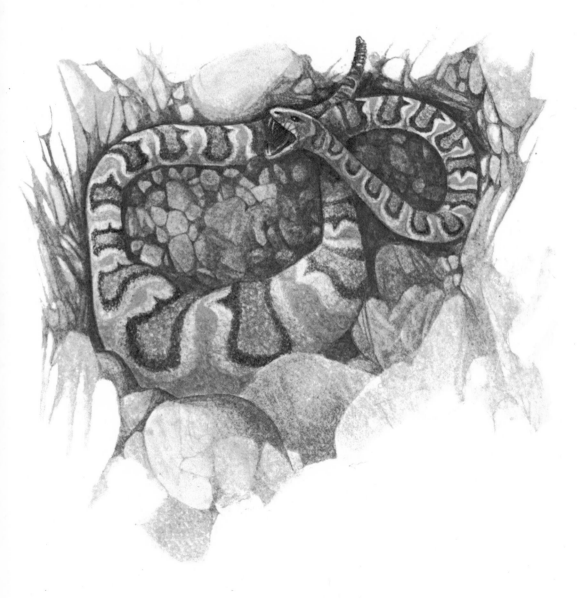

*The Navajo people like to use poetry
and art in their daily life and work,
and in their dances and ceremonies.
This imaginative story tells how they
learned the ceremonies in which they plead
or give thanks for rain, a great blessing
in their life.*

The Water Maiden of the Navajo

There was once a Navajo Indian whose name was Man-with-a-Rock-Shirt, who lived near the Chol'i'i mountain, which was near a canyon. He was a strong man and a good hunter.

One day while hunting he became thirsty, and so he went to the river to drink. As he came near the water, he saw a baby swimming in and out among the rocks. For a long time he stood and watched. Then he went home.

The Navajo wondered about that child. He decided to return to the same place the next day, at the same time, to see if it was there again.

Yes, there was the child swimming again. He went home, deciding to return on the morrow and do something.

The next day he went to the river, and seeing some tall grass at the edge of the water, he hid there. Soon the child came swimming by. It floated and splashed and played.

When the babe came near the edge, the Navajo jumped into the water, took the child in his arms, and ran to the shore and up the nearby hill.

He stopped at the top and looked behind. There was the river water rearing high and falling toward him.

So the man ran down the other side of the hill and did not stop until he came to his hogan.

When his wife saw the child, she was very glad, for they had none of their own. And when she found it was a girl, she was even more happy.

They dearly loved the child, and she brought much joy to their home.

When the girl was thirteen years old, she made her first cake, and the first Maiden Ceremony was held over her. But after that she would not touch food or water.

"Why don't you eat or drink?" the parents asked.

"Mother, Father, I want to go back to my own country."

They were much surprised, for they thought she did not know from where she had come.

The man said, "You are right, my daughter. I found you in the water, and if you want to go back to the water, it is our wish too."

The next morning she went away and at night she came back.

"Where were you, our daughter?" the parents asked.

"I went to the water and there I heard someone chopping wood," she answered. "I went up the hill and looked, but I did not see anyone. Then the noise stopped and I looked all over for tracks, but I could not find any."

The next morning she went off again and heard the same sounds, but when she came near the water they stopped. She looked again for tracks but there were none.

On the third morning her father gave her a basket of holy stones. There were chips of beads, turquoise, white shells, black jet, and red stones. Over them he sprinkled a shining mineral. On that he sprinkled pollen from cattails and blue water iris. Then he put the finest crystals he could find along the shore over the pollen.

The girl went to the river. She heard the chopping noise, and when she came near the waters she saw a blue ax standing against a stump, and she thought she saw someone move.

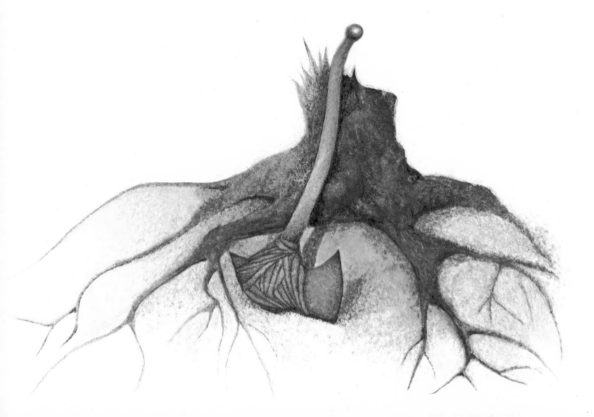

Right then the river opened. The water rose like a blanket, and out of it stepped a tall young man.

"What are you doing here?" asked the young man. "This is not a place for Earth People."

"I have wanted to come to this place for a long time."

"Are you the one who was taken from the river when you were very young?" he asked.

"Yes, and I have always wanted to come back."

"Then come with me," the young man said.

He rolled the river back like a blanket and there was a path, which they followed. On the path there were tracks of a water horse that had hoofs like a cow.

The Water Person took the maiden to the home of the Water Buffalo, who was the Holy One in the river, and she gave him the basket with the sacred stones.

"It is a pleasing gift," Water Buffalo said, "and now I

will give you a gift to take back to the Earth People."

He took some buffalo chips and some hair from his forehead and sides. He took the oozy earth from under the water and put on it froth from his mouth. He took water from the four rains and the four vapors. All of it he placed in a medicine bag and, giving it to the girl, he said, "This will be your helping medicine and must be used by Earth People when they want rain. You, daughter, will be the head of a new clan and your descendants will be known as the Sacred People. Snakes and lightning will never harm you. But for this, two of your descendants must come back to me."

Then he instructed her how to make a special hogan for the Rain Ceremony and how to do the ceremonial dance.

"Now, go back to the Earth People and teach them."

The maiden went back to the Earth People and became a mother and grandmother of many children. She taught them all the Rain Ceremony with the special dance and the special medicine.

The Earth People planted corn in the canyon. It ripened and from it came rich ears with golden tassels.

One day the Earth People sent a boy and a girl to the canyon. Suddenly they saw a flood coming over them. They shouted to the children to come back, but the flood carried them away without even touching the cornfields.

The two children were taken underwater to the home of the Holy One, the Water Buffalo, as he had predicted. And the Earth People kept the good rains, and the ceremonies and dances.

The Algonquin Indians told this lovely story about the wind. They enjoy poetic stories about nature and told this gentle one many times.

South Wind and His Golden-haired Love

South Wind, Shawondasee, was a lazy person. He moved slowly and liked watching the pink blossoms fall from the trees.

One day while lazying through the air, he saw a beautiful maiden with golden hair standing on the Western Prairie.

He loved her and wanted to marry her, but she was far away and he was too lazy to fly to her and tell her. "I'll go tomorrow," he said.

Each day he saw her and said . . . "tomorrow." There was always a new tomorrow, and though every day she looked lovelier and lovelier he was always too lazy to go to her.

"The next day," he said.

Then one morning when he went to look for his golden-haired love, she was not there. Yes, she was there, but now her golden hair was silver-white!

"Ah, my brother North Wind has come and put frost on her lovely golden hair."

Shawondasee was sad and heaved a great, deep sigh. And when his sigh reached the maiden, her silver hair began to float through the air and . . . she was gone!

Some say it was not an Indian maiden, but Dandelion, whom Shawondasee thought was an Indian maiden when he saw her from a great distance.

PRONUNCIATION GUIDE

How Corn Came to the Indians
Mondahmin	MOHN dah min
Ojibwa	oh CHIP wah
Wunzh	wunch

Honeyed Words Can't Sweeten Evil
| Algonquin | al GON kin |

Ma'nabus
| Ma'nabus | mah NAH bush |
| Menominee | meh NOM in ee |

The Great Father Mosquito
| Tuscarora | tus kah ROH rah |

The Sad Marriage of North
| Cherokee | CHEHR oh kee |

The Adventures of the Seneca Chief
| Heno | hay NOH |
| Seneca | SEN eh kah |

The Song That Comes from the Sea
Biloxi	bee LOK see
Choctaw	CHOK taw
Pascagoula	pas kah GOO lah

The Cranes of the Great Lakes
| Quapaw | KWAH pah |

Gluska'be, the Penobscot Hero

Gluska'be	GLOOS kah bay
Penobscot	peh NOB skut

In the Beginning

Zuñi	ZOON yee

How Rabbit Got the Best of Coyote

Sia	ZEE ah

In the Days of the Great Buffalo

Comanche	koh MAN chee

Kwi-na the Eagle

I'-o-wi	EE oh wee
Kwi-na	KWEE nah
O-ho-tcu	oh HOH choo
To-go'-a	toh GOH ah
Tso-a-vwits	TSOH ahv witz
U-ja	OO jah
Ute	yoot

The Water Maiden of the Navajo

Chol' i' i	CHOHL ee ee
Navajo	NAH vah hoh

South Wind and His Golden-haired Love

Algonquin	al GON kin
Shawondasee	shah wun DAH see

1 2 3 4 5 6 7—U—82 81 80 79 78